Post-Limerence

J. Hyde T.

BookLeaf Publishing

India | USA | UK

Presentation by *BookLeaf Publishing*

Web: www.bookleafpub.com

E-mail: info@bookleafpub.com

ISBN: 9789360948566

First edition 2024

To all that will be visiting Rock Bottom's basement. May it be one hell of a bounce.

PREFACE

This collection of poems explores the intricacy of what can be gained from the inconsistent forms of losses and missed opportunities.

for him.

I'm scared of myself at night
when I'm awake in bed afraid to fall asleep

as the tumultuous silence wraps around me
I wonder why you didn't call
or even text that night

Was I not enough to hear your final cry
but only enough to be the one to see you
laying there still in your chair
not coming out of your greatest high

if you were trying to prove a point
you clearly won
it pains me every day that I have to breathe for
two instead of one

every smile I make now feels like it could've
been with you
and every time I sit in my chair
I wished that I never woke up to discovering
that you were no longer you.

eres.

On my strolls, my eyes would go on these long walks
walks

I would be unable to focus as the sinuous sea
makes its way onto land
flooding my mind with fleeting images of you
warm, as incandescent lights
where the filament flickers as I am reminded of
your hair
gently caressing your cheeks
loosely tugged behind your ears
leading me to the nape of your neck

as the waves makes its way to my chest
I can hear your breath brush upon my face
pulling me farther from verity

your smile, the curling of your lips
the gentle tug of your shoulders
a growing fervor in my heart
where I am ashamed that such allure
only shows itself

when I am on a stroll
and my eyes go on their long walk.

for when my homies want to be more than bromies.

Now all I can do is cross out each sentence
until I run out of ink

black out each line that has your name
so the grasp beneath my pinky is spoiled to the
tone of grey

had I known how hard it would be to rid of you
I would've used a pencil
so I can seek the aid of an eraser
to have it reveal the indentations you've creased
onto my skin

I wish I can tear off these pages
remove the part of me that is so, so close to you
as I lay in the sea waiting for the wound to seal

but instead, I'm left with this heartache
hoping that the last page in my book
would still be filled by you.

i have no idea what i'd be doing today or tomorrow.

Cuff my hands
cause I'm so fucking tired of everyone telling
me what I should do
how I should do it
and when I should do it

I've been living more than half my life for you
and the other half less of you

Maybe if you followed through
and doubled down on drawing lines on my back
I might've been something

Now I'm less of a person
more a collection of flaws and loose ends

My mind has been so loaded the past few years
no lost and found
can hold all of me

You don't remember when I got sick,
nor how much guilt I felt when I walked away
from the car accident

Your first question wasn't if I was okay
but if it was my fault

I didn't tell you
because I thought you already knew

I'm a fuck up
on meto and cyclone
for my failing heart.

I'm living a chapter

with the end waiting for me

and I can't say I'm scared.

one bed.

there are brilliantly colored magazines
where all that should be beautiful occupy the
spine in between
and everyone's differences are separated by the
page
only intertwining momentarily to outlined
quotas

their ingenuine smiles
strike like stretches of underpasses beneath
freeways
dividing the lively from the deadly
where cars roam freely
and the children with dreams saunter carelessly

they too can be something
but we're all sheeps dressed as adults
crossing the bridge to play pretend
unnecessary saviors
explaining the lack of well behavior is the
downfall to them all

that them crossing the bridge to turn on the
lights

to diners and laced up establishments is their
duty and their fault

it's a two-way overpass
traveled most by one

your kid's school is two blocks and a divergence
away
but private school is an option
where their influences come from the insane
instead of experiences that could've been shared
with the slow, growing motions
questioned to be too dangerous and mundane

I hope you.
-we know,
when the sun sets
and the night sky breaks

we all can only sleep on one bed

all vulnerable. the same.

soured.

Sometimes I lose myself in my dream
where the deep sea has made its way
to city blocks to drown the last harvest
off an Autumn losing its glow

I would be knee deep in the cold
listening to cars churning and their owners'
breath wading away with the wind
as uncertainty grows

I would walk to lower grounds
so my neck can greet the great blue
before whispering

"I told you so,
you should've let me take swimming lessons."

Truly, I am happy your answer was always no
because two more steps
my lungs would be filled with an overwhelming
greed

Another two
my eyes would remain closed
to this soiree of sorrow

peace

and the notion of fortune
emanating in a restaurant party room
suddenly feels less as a burden.

the radiator is off.

I used to sit in front of the TV,
pretending to understand The Simpsons

I used to sit in front of the TV,
and play with my quarter capsule toys

I used to sit in front of the TV,
pretending to not worry about the dark

I used to sit in front of the TV,
and wonder when I'd be eating dinner

I used to sit in front of the TV,
pretending to enjoy the silence

I used to sit in front of the TV,
and ask why I'm always alone

I used to sit in front of the TV,
waiting for someone to come home

mentiras.

I'm tired of these walks
where leaves and snow would come in for their
seasonal meet and greet
before shedding and feathering away

where footprints always change
smiles turn to pain
breathing never felt more piercing
this lingering regret
the myriad source of all that was in vain

I remember the buses and the trains missing
each other by
minutes
to watch the rain
waltz in truculent silence
wreaking havoc
to the rhythmic stain on
my heart

I'm tired of remembering
walks by buses and trains
where I scream in mute
where all that falls arrest me slowly
where the thought of you
has me going insane

carbon monoxide.

The alarm went off that night
as the radiator whistled

My vision was blurred, hands unsteady
bottles empty
head on my table, breath on a train ride
delayed indefinitely

The ringing caught me from sliding
I was tired, floating on water, knowing I can't
swim
feeling lost in absolute

My thoughts bled down my skin
sweaty as the sidewalk pavements

I wasn't scared nor at peace
just waiting for the moment as I pulled the
batteries
drove myself to bed
ready to try myself with Fate

Only to wake up
disappointed
to an alarm going off
aimlessly

chemo terminal.

it dripped down my nose nonchalantly
felt like a runny nose
from watching the first snow fall
shirtless in the cold

that weight in my head
when I realized the ruby stains on my thumbs
were my body's way of calling for help
left me still on my chair

it happened again
too many nights
I was ready to abandon it all

the images of them
sending me off
roped me with guilt

I was gone for 8 months
a fight I didn't want to win
if I could've leaned out
I would've gone for a swim
and taken the deepest breath
to saturate my lungs

but sinking down the sea
would've been the easy way out

I was a dumbass for pain
seeking validation from neglect

and I'm glad
when I was through

this was nothing more
than an 8-hour Greyhound ride.

hives.

I wish I never woke up
because your silence is so fucking loud

it should've been me
who was taken out
it should've been me
who flatlined

I really hate this day
it comes once a year
but the wrecking noise
haunts me daily

your love one's cry
their tears that it wasn't my demise
left a permanent knot on my throat

every time I drink
I choke knowing
my breath should've
gone to you.

tus labios son hermosos.

I want to burn
I want to engulf
char the forest except for one

With you I'm contained
an ignition unlearned
I merely spark
only to land momentarily on stones

To watch you thrive
for seconds
I'm alive

I'm cold
I'm scared
Your touch, of all, warms me,
a stray, portraying the role of a flame

I don't deserve these moments
or the idea we can be together
where you cannot get hurt

You're not as endless as air
You're timeless and near
I'm a relentless fire

who burns and engulfs all

even the ones I care.

you fell for me. i fell for you harder. you left.

If I can see you again
I'll lean in and etch your face into my eyes

Go for a long walk along the copse
let the air caress me as I undress
the static lingering by my ears
to hear your vibrant voice
your heart-melting laugh

I've become a prisoner to your rhythm
your floaty gestures
touches of elusiveness
that will revisit me at night
reminding me the scars that once stung
will heal and be soft to touch

My hands have been reaching for yours
unsteadily ready
to catch you
to embrace you if you were to lose balance
walking along the curbs
and fall

My everything, my all

everything you've come to ignore
when I fell harder
to you closing the last draw

My end, your hair
a grasp of sand I hold dear
to my hands
to my feet
I've been yours all along

Your distance, mi amor
a performance of clashes and flaws
to your smile
to your eyes
your thoughts of me
has always been wrong.

she was clothed in my dreams.

Life is boring
the bittersweet soiree I enjoy in my mouth
the elegiac smell of coffee has come to bore

It's not bad
like how I would still be content from
the steam off of freshly cooked rice
the same dishes I always eat

the memories I cherish so much
will still be tuned to repeat

But somewhere when all was happening
the runners high became just running

Underdogs of every movie
were winners before their climactic dance

Pollen collection became a mundane chore
Honey making dripped without guilt

A familiar comfort
like the stretch of unfamiliar roads all mapped
out by Google

to reach a bed by night

And if I were asked

"Would you live this way again, if you were
given another chance?"

I would answer.

Yes.

Because she was clothed in my dreams.

eyes on me.

sit down
let me pour you a cup of tea
in this 90-degree weather

entertain me
write out another story
for you and me

enlist us on another travel
along the sea
deep in the forest
amongst the clouds

tell me more stories
where you and me
could be

sit down
let me pour you a cup of hot tea
in this frigid weather

talk to me

tell me you cannot see beyond me
where you and me

may never be

sit down
let me give you my cup of tea
in this space that has unfold
between you and me

remind me
about our stories
that we
will never see.

i wish you'd call.

it has been over a year
since we've last spoke
you used to call me
mindless banters
unrehearsed
picked right up
from where we paused

I thought it was work
or you were catching up with life
you withdrew
from all that I knew

closed your accounts
changed your number
moved across town
left no trace behind

if I did something wrong
I wish to apologize
but you're unfounded

now and then
I drive by a sound
that reminds me of you

our weekend excursions
our lackluster walks
to satisfy our late-night cravings

all now just faded memories

I still miss you
maybe if I see you
we'll start again
but this time from a stop
where I will have to learn
to trust you
again.

departing flight #011.
(jimmy's mom.)

I know you're safe and sound
Slow dancing in the limelight
Making long distance calls to my mom
Asking for forgiveness
When I'm here glaring right at you

Hey. Carl.
Why are you doing this to me?
Putting me on hold
I'm splitting white lines at the intersection
squeezing fruity pebbles out my nose
waiting for the kids to drop by
saying, "Silly Wabbit, Trix are for kids"
But I'm already on Tony
riding the rainbow
and your words are spinning
like snowflakes
stuck in a snow globe
clawing at my cheeks

Fuck you. Carl.
For not dialing the exit code
and deciding it's my voice that speaks
But when I look at me

I see you
My chest goes and run loops
French kissing a paper bag
Screaming

"DAD, DAD, DAD, DAD, DEAD."

Hello, Carl?
It's me. I'm fucking you.
Is that why you're fucking me, too?

Bye. Carl.
Carl. Bye.

these voices are real.

I memorized the jingles to your keys
Your heavy
       footsteps
           that reiterated
     your underwhelming
presence

I would greet you with my high-strung eyes
having caught reruns of Seinfeld and Friends

-my first run-in with Carl-

His hands hit different.
Warmer than yours.

Your voice would hitch a ride with the steam off
the rice cooker

but it always came landing like a shovel
clanging on a wok

As comprehensible as laugh tracks
that Carl would laugh along with

when he ran into me.

And I would just chew
taper off each of my words with a smile

waiting for you to fill up the bathtub

And Carl would always exhale,
before screaming

CUT.
GOOD TAKE.

So I could finally close my eyes
lay my head in water
to relieve myself of your affectation

TAKE A BREAK.

from you gassing me up
as you crown yourself with modesty
for having perused a mother's playbook

But nothing would fill the obstreperous silence
as much as Carl's stories
of him walking on double solid yellow lines
and chasing smog trails
where he'd hope to walk onto pedestrian
crossing
to somehow become

one again

and I would nod to you bloviating
feeling like Guilt standing outdoors
peering through glass during daytime
unsure if you're the reflection

of what I am.

or who I am.

at your expense.

Why are your shoulders like that?
Is it from the weight you pulled aside
when you told her I've got a plan?

I don't.

My ambition has left to grab some milk
I have his keys
we don't even have a doorbell

I buckle a little every time you pass by
knowing when you return
I would still be here
ponzi fueling your trust in me
cause you've lost another day to aging
for me to just stare at walls

I've heard it all
claims that my thirties will cover up my flaws
but I'm tired in my twenties
worried that you'd fall
and I wouldn't even be able to catch you
let alone support you

I want to get on my knees

but asking for forgiveness doesn't mean shit.
since you could've stood tall

if maybe

I wasn't here at all.

in the next slice.

in this loaf
we were near

if sandwiches were made
with slices of bread pulled disorderly
maybe we would've met earlier
be held together by everything in between us
that we cared so much about

in the next loaf
I won't forget that you've once walked with me
I won't forget how well we fit next to each other

in the next loaf
I'll be sure to wait for you
jump into the sunlight and soak up the warmth
for you

in the next loaf
I'll hold your hands when you're cold
put my coat over you and walk you home

in the next loaf
I'll keep my voice and laughter to myself
so when I finally find you

I will spend it all on you

in the next loaf
I know I'll settle down with you
start a family, raise two

but in this loaf
we were near

with a slice
in between.

for her.

when you laid there on the hospital bed

I cried in your motions
unable to keep up with your pace
the pain you had in your head
what I couldn't see

but your muted screams

I felt

roping senseless words around my neck

I tiptoed around you
tongue-tied to the best memories of you

I'm always a few days off
unable to recall
because the handles
had me on call

when I sat down
to understand the headaches in me
were less than yours
and my time couldn't quite keep up with you

that yesterday and today
didn't equate to tomorrow

an anguish downpour saturated my bare skin
reminding me that we come and go with nothing

I'm tormented that I can't leave with you

but I'm happy that your end
was quiet and still.